The Rourke Guide
to State Symbols

BIRDS

Jason Cooper

The Rourke Press, Inc.
Vero Beach, Florida 32964

PHOTO CREDITS:
p. 45, 46 (WI) © Deborah Allen; p. 5, 7, 8, 10, 11, 13 (GA), 15, 17, 18, 21, 22 (MD), 26 (MO), 28, 29, 30, 31, 33, 36 (PA), 38, 39 (TN), 43, 44 © Tom Ulrich; p.9, 14 © Gary Kramer; cover, p. 16 (IL), 19, 22 (MA), 32 (NY), 40, 42 © Tom Vezo; p. 25, 34, 35, 36 (OR) © Steve Bentsen; p. 32 (NC) © Laura Elaine Moore; p. 26 (MT), 27, 47 © Cary Given; p. 6, 7, 16 (IN), 20, 23, 24, 39 (SD), 41, 46 (WV) © Lynn M. Stone; p.37 courtesy Rhode Island Tourism Division; p. 12 (DE) courtesy Delaware Department of Tourism

COVER ART: James Spence

EDITORIAL SERVICES:
Penworthy Learning Systems

Library of Congress Cataloging-in-Publication Data

Cooper, Jason, 1942 -
  Birds / Jason Cooper.
    p. cm. — (The Rourke guide to state symbols)
  Includes index.
  Summary: Describes the different birds that have been chosen by the fifty states and the District of Columbia to represent them.
  ISBN 1-57103-192-8
  1. State birds—United States—Juvenile literature. [1. State birds. 2. Birds. 3. Emblems, State.]
I. Title II. Series: Cooper, Jason, 1942 - The Rourke guide to state symbols.
QL682.C67 1997
598' .0973—dc21   97–16920
                                                CIP
                                               AC

Printed in the USA

TABLE OF CONTENTS

INTRODUCTION

America chose the bald eagle, a large, powerful bird of prey, as its national bird in the late 1700's. Years later (1927) Florida, first to choose a state bird, chose the mockingbird. Since then all the other 49 states and the District of Columbia have chosen state birds. None of the choices were birds of prey, however. Small songbirds were selected by forty states, along with a few game birds and waterfowl, while two states (Rhode Island and Delaware) chose barnyard birds (red hen and blue hen).

States brag about the things that set them apart from each other. Where state birds are concerned, though, many states have been content to follow the lead of others. The redbird, or cardinal, mockingbird, and western meadowlark were the most popular choices, together representing 18 states.

Most birds are not "loyal" to one state. They often travel great distances. An exception is Hawaii's state bird, the nene (nay-nay), or Hawaiian goose. This rare bird is found nowhere but Hawaii and Maui.

Many birds were chosen for their lilting voice or brilliant colors. Others, like the black-capped chickadee, have become favorites by visiting home feeders, or by having some special link with a state's history.

Of the 600 species of wild birds living in the United States, 27 kinds represent states and the District of Columbia. These honored birds, plus the American eagle, remind us that all birds are beautiful and fascinating creatures.

ALABAMA

COMMON FLICKER (YELLOWHAMMER)

Scientific Name: *Colaptes auratus*

Length: 12 - 14 inches (30 - 35 centimeters)

Year Made State Bird: 1927

Despite the name "flicker" Alabama's state bird is a woodpecker. Unlike most woodpeckers, however, flickers often feed on the ground instead of on tree trunks. Ants are a favorite food of flickers.

Old-time Alabamans said the flicker's gray cap reminded them of the state's Confederate soldiers in uniform during the American Civil War.

The underside of the flicker's wings, easily seen when the bird flies, are bright yellow.

ALASKA
WILLOW PTARMIGAN

Scientific Name: *Lagopus lagopus*
Length: 16 inches (40 centimeters)
Year Made State Bird: 1955

Alaska's state bird, the willow ptarmigan, is a plump, bright-eyed game bird with a loud, clattering call. The ptarmigan belongs to the grouse family, like Pennsylvania's ruffed grouse, or partridge (see p. 36).

Willow ptarmigan survive Alaska's cold, snowy winters by burrowing under snow and eating seeds and berries.

Ptarmigan are brownish in summer and hide easily in their surroundings. In winter they also blend into their surroundings—by turning white!

ARIZONA
CACTUS WREN

Scientific Name: *Campylorhrnchus brunneicapillus*
Length: 7 - 8 1/2 inches (18 - 21 centimeters)
Year Made State Bird: 1931

Arizona's cactus wren is the largest American wren. The cactus wren easily tiptoes among the cacti without getting speared.

The cactus wren builds several nests in the thorny plants of Arizona. Each nest has a tunnel-like entrance. Unlike most birds, the cactus wren uses one or more of its nests year round.

ARKANSAS
MOCKINGBIRD

Scientific Name: *Mimus polyglottos*
Length: 9 - 11 inches (23 - 28 centimeters)
Year Made State Bird: 1929

Arkansas was the third of five southern states that chose the mockingbird as its state bird. The mockingbird is found throughout much of the eastern United States, but it is most common in the Southeast.

The mockingbird is related to the thrashers and catbird. As a singer, though, the mockingbird is in a class by itself. People love the mocker's music and ability to imitate other birds.

(See Florida, p. 12; Mississippi, p. 25; Tennessee, p. 39; and Texas, p. 40.)

CALIFORNIA
CALIFORNIA QUAIL

Scientific Name: *Callipepla californica*
Length: 10 1/2 inches (27 centimeters)
Year Made State Bird: 1931

California quail are popular with California birdwatchers and bird hunters alike. The males are particularly handsome with their long head plumes and white trim.

Quail travel in flocks. They feed on the ground, and they prefer to walk or run rather than fly. When frightened, they take off in low, fast flight with a loud whirring of wings.

California quail live mostly in low, brushy country. In summer, though, flocks of quail move onto mountain slopes as high as 5,000 feet (1,524 meters) above sea level.

COLORADO
LARK BUNTING

Scientific Name: *Calamospiza melanocorys*
Length: 7 inches (18 centimeters)
Year Made State Bird: 1931

Lark bunting is named for its song, which reminds listeners of the clear, sweet song of larks.

Buntings are members of the sparrow family. The female lark bunting's brown-striped feathers are much like a sparrow's. Her mate, however, is boldly marked in black and white during the spring and summer.

In late fall, when lark buntings fly south from Colorado to warmer regions, the male's black feathers are replaced by brown ones.

CONNECTICUT
AMERICAN ROBIN

Scientific Name: *Turdus migratorius*
Length: 9 - 11 inches (23 - 28 centimeters)
Year Made State Bird: 1943

The American robin is one of the most familiar and loved of all American birds. Three states—Connecticut, Michigan (p. 23), and Wisconsin (p. 46)—chose it for their state bird.

Each March the cheery calls of robins announce the beginning of spring in the North. In October, robins fly south, marking the start of autumn.

DELAWARE

BLUE HEN (OLD ENGLISH GAME HEN)

Scientific Name: *Gallus domesticus*
Weight: 4 - 5 pounds
   (1.8 - 2.3 kilograms)
Year Made State Bird: 1939

   The "blue hen" is a bluish variety of the Old English game hen. This bird is a breed of chicken developed for fighting. Fights between the fearless roosters of the breed were common "sport" in Colonial America. The toughness and courage of Delaware's fighting men against British soldiers were compared to that of the fighting roosters.

   Very few people raise the blue variety of game hen, even in Delaware. Rooster fights are illegal now, but the game hens are sometimes still used for show.

FLORIDA

MOCKINGBIRD

Scientific Name:
   Mimus polyglottos
Length: 9 - 11 inches
   (23 - 28 centimeters)
Year Made State Bird:
   1907

(Florida continued)

Florida, in 1907, became the first of five states to name the mockingbird as its state bird.

The mockingbird is famous in Florida, and elsewhere, for its ability to mimic, or copy, the songs of other birds. Most of the mockingbird's music, however, is its own.
(See Arkansas, p. 8; Mississippi, p. 25; Tennessee, p. 39; and Texas, p. 40)

GEORGIA
BROWN THRASHER

Scientific Name:
   Toxostoma rufum
Length: 11 1/2 inches
   (29 centimeters)
Year Made State Bird:
   1970

A cousin of the mockingbird, the brown thrasher, too, is a fine songster.

With its mostly brown back and tail, the brown thrasher hides easily among dry leaves and undergrowth where it hunts insects.

The brown thrasher tends to scatter leaves about as it hunts. That habit may be the reason it earned the name "thrasher."

HAWAII
HAWAIIAN GOOSE (NENE)

Scientific Name: *Branta sandvicensis*
Length: 22 - 28 inches (56 - 71 centimeters)
Year Made State Bird: 1957

Hawaii's state bird is one of the rarest birds in the world. Only a few hundred Hawaiian geese survive in the wild.

The Hawaiian goose's tameness nearly caused its extinction. When British sailors first reached Hawaii more than 200 years ago, they slaughtered the geese for food. More recently, free-roaming cats, dogs, pigs, and mongooses have been the bird's greatest enemies.

Hawaiian geese seldom swim. Their open, grassy habitat on volcanic slopes is nearly water-free. The geese take moisture from the plants they eat.

IDAHO
MOUNTAIN BLUEBIRD

Scientific Name: *Sialia currucoides*
Length: 7 inches (18 centimeters)
Year Made State Bird: 1931

The male mountain bluebird is a blue beauty during the spring and summer. It is more completely feathered in blue than its cousin, the eastern bluebird.

The mountain bluebird nests in tree hollows, often using a hole hammered out by a woodpecker. Western bluebird lovers can often attract the mountain bluebird to their birdhouses.

(See Nevada, p. 28.)

ILLINOIS
CARDINAL

Scientific Name:
  Cardinalis cardinalis
Length: 7 1/2 - 9 inches
  (19 - 23 centimeters)
Year Made State Bird:
  1929

Illinois is one of seven states to choose the beloved cardinal as its state bird.

The male cardinal is one of the most beautiful of North American song birds. Its red feathers, black "mustache," and perky crest make the familiar redbird unmistakable.

Both male and female cardinals sing as nesting time approaches.

(See Indiana, p. 16; Kentucky, p. 19; North Carolina, p. 32; Ohio, p. 34; Virginia, p. 43; and West Virginia, p. 46.)

INDIANA
CARDINAL

Scientific Name:
  Cardinalis cardinalis
Length: 7 1/2 - 9 inches
  (19-23 centimeters)
Year Made State Bird:
  1933

(Indiana continued)

Indiana springs are made brighter each year by the state bird—the northern cardinal. Everyone enjoys the bright flash of red wherever the male cardinal goes. The cardinal's clear spring whistle—*whoit, whoit, whoit, cheer, cheer, cheer*—is also delightful.

(See Illinois, p. 16; Kentucky, p. 19; North Carolina, p. 32; Ohio, p. 34; Virginia, p. 43; and West Virginia, p. 46.)

IOWA
AMERICAN GOLDFINCH

Scientific Name:
  Carduelis tristis
Length: 5 inches
  (13 centimeters)
Year Made State Bird:
  1933

The goldfinch is America's "wild canary" or "yellowbird." The female goldfinch is more olive-colored, though, than yellow. The male goldfinch wears strikingly handsome yellow and black plumage in summer. In autumn, the male's feathers fade to dull yellow and brown.

The goldfinch live throughout the 48 mainland states.
(See New Jersey, p. 30; and Washington, p. 44.)

KANSAS
WESTERN MEADOWLARK

Scientific Name: *Sturnella neglecta*
Length: 9 inches (23 centimeters)
Year Made State Bird: 1937

Meadowlarks are truly birds of field and meadow. The western meadowlark, the state bird of Kansas and five other states, lives throughout the western U.S. and eastward into Indiana, Kentucky, Tennessee, Alabama, and the Florida panhandle.

The western meadowlark often perches on fence posts and warbles its song in a clear, flutelike voice.
(See Montana,p. 26; Nebraska, p. 27; North Dakota, p. 33; Oregon, p. 36; and Wyoming, p. 47.)

KENTUCKY
CARDINAL

Scientific Name: *Cardinalis cardinalis*
Length: 7 1/2 - 9 inches (19 - 23 centimeters)
Year Made State Bird: 1926

In 1926, Kentucky was the first state to choose the cardinal as its state bird. Over the next 24 years, six more states made the cardinal their official state bird.

The bright male cardinal is rarely seen without its gray-feathered mate. Even during the winter months, pairs of cardinals are often seen together.

(See Illinois and Indiana, p. 16; North Carolina, p. 32; Ohio, p. 34; Virginia, p. 43; and West Virginia, p. 46.)

LOUISIANA
BROWN PELICAN

Scientific Name: *Pelecanus occidentalis*
Length: 50 inches (127 centimeters)
Year Made State Bird: 1966

Louisiana's state bird, the brown pelican, is the largest of the official state birds. It's also the only one that's a feathered fisherman.

Brown pelicans live on a fish diet. They often dive headlong into the ocean for their prey.

Brown pelicans live along the coasts of Louisiana and other southern states. Brown pelicans are returning to Louisiana in great numbers after nearly disappearing from the state in the 1960's and 1970's. The pelicans were being poisoned by DDT, a chemical that washed into the sea.

MAINE

BLACK-CAPPED CHICKADEE

Scientific Name: *Parus atricapillus*
Length: 4 3/4 - 5 3/4 inches (12 - 14 centimeters)
Year Made State Bird: 1927

The little black-capped chickadee is tame and trusting. It's a favorite bird at winter feeders in Maine and across Canada and the northern United States. Black-capped chickadees love suet and sunflower seeds.

The black-capped chickadee's close cousin, the boreal chickadee, also lives in Maine. Its cap, back, and sides are brown.
(See Massachusetts, p. 22.)

MARYLAND
NORTHERN ORIOLE (BALTIMORE ORIOLE)

Scientific Name:
Icterus galbula
Length: 7 - 8 inches
(18 - 20 centimeters)
Year Made State Bird:
1947

The male northern oriole, often called the Baltimore oriole in the East, is a brilliantly colored bird. Its colors matched the family colors of the Baltimore family, who colonized Maryland. For some time, the Colonists knew the oriole as "Baltimore-bird."

The oriole was also known in the early days of America as the "fiery hang nest." The words "hang nest" referred to the oriole's baglike nest.

MASSACHUSETTS
BLACK-CAPPED CHICKADEE

Scientific Name:
Parus atricapillus
Length:
4 3/4 - 5 3/4 inches
(12 - 14 centimeters)
Year Made State Bird:
1941

(Massachusetts continued)

The black-capped chickadee, the state bird of both Maine (p. 21) and Massachusetts, is something of an acrobat with wings. Because it can grip a branch while upside down, it finds insects even on the underside of branches.

The chickadee was named for its dark cap and call: *chick-a-dee-dee-dee.*

MICHIGAN
AMERICAN ROBIN

Scientific Name:
   Turdus migratorius
Length: 9 - 11 inches
   (23 - 28 centimeters)
Year Made State Bird:
   1931

The robin's brick-red vest is a familiar sight on Michigan lawns. Robins love earthworms and grubs, which they pluck from beneath the grass. Robins also eat berries, and they are especially fond of cherries.

(See Connecticut, p. 11; and Wisconsin, p. 46.)

MINNESOTA
COMMON LOON

Scientific Name: *Gavia immer*
Length: 28 - 36 inches (about 70 - 90 centimeters)
Year Made State Bird: 1961

Minnesota is a state with several thousand lakes. No wonder it made the handsome common loon its state bird!

During the summer nesting season, the loon is a lake bird. Each pair of loons "claims" a lake, or large section of it, and defends it against other loons. The loons build a lakeshore nest and raise their chicks on fish they catch by diving.

The loon's wild, haunting cry is summer music in Minnesota's lake country.

MISSISSIPPI
MOCKINGBIRD

Scientific Name: *Mimus polyglottos*
Length: 9 - 11 inches (23 - 28 centimeters)
Year Made State Bird: 1944

Mississippi was the last of five states to make the mockingbird its state bird.

Mockingbirds are quite at home among houses and yards. Their singing often lasts well into the night and begins again before dawn.

(See Arkansas, p. 8; Florida, p. 12; Tennessee, p. 39; and Texas, p. 40.)

MISSOURI
EASTERN BLUEBIRD

Scientific Name: *Sialia sialis*
Length: 7 inches
    (18 centimeters)
Year Made State Bird: 1927

  With a pretty voice and even prettier plumage, the eastern bluebird is a favorite wherever it lives. It has been Missouri's official state bird since 1927.

  The bluebird likes roadside trees, orchards, and open woodlands. It nests in old woodpecker holes in trees and in birdboxes.
(See New York, p. 32.)

MONTANA
WESTERN MEADOWLARK

Scientific Name:
    Sturnella neglecta
Length: 9 inches
    (23 centimeters)
Year Made State Bird:
    1931

(Montana continued)

In Montana and other Western states, the meadowlark is as familiar as the prairie grass. Just about everyone recognizes this yellow-breasted bird with the black, V-shaped feather vest and cheery song.

(See Kansas, p. 18; Nebraska, p. 27; North Dakota, p. 33; Oregon, p. 36; and Wyoming, p. 47.)

NEBRASKA
WESTERN MEADOWLARK

Scientific Name:
Sturnella neglecta
Length: 9 inches
(23 centimeters)
Year Made State Bird:
1929

Two kinds of meadowlarks live in Nebraska—the eastern and the western. The official state bird is the western meadowlark, but they are difficult to tell from the eastern meadowlarks until they sing.

The western bird has a richer, more musical call than its cousin. Otherwise, the two kinds of meadowlarks are very much alike.

(See Kansas, p. 18; Montana, p. 26; North Dakota, p. 33; Oregon, p. 36; and Wyoming, p. 47.)

NEVADA
MOUNTAIN BLUEBIRD

Scientific Name: *Sialia currucoides*
Length: 7 inches (18 centimeters)
Year Made State Bird: 1967

The male mountain bluebird flashes like a turquoise light. Its mate, though, is brown, with just a hint of blue in her plumage.

Mountain bluebirds like high country. They live in mountain ranges up to 10,000 feet (3,048 meters) above sea level.

Mountain bluebirds live far beyond the borders of Nevada. They can be found in North to Central Alaska, south to Southern California, and east into Oklahoma. (See Idaho, p. 15.)

NEW HAMPSHIRE
PURPLE FINCH

Scientific Name: *Carpodacus purpureus*
Length: 5 1/2 - 6 inches (14 - 15 centimeters)
Year Made State Bird: 1957

The purple finch is a familiar little bird in New Hampshire and throughout much of the eastern United States.

Purple finches are not really purple. The males have some reddish-pink plumage, however. The females are buff-colored and brown.

Purple finches like evergreen forests. During the winter, they are regular visitors to bird feeders. They especially like sunflower seeds.

NEW JERSEY
AMERICAN GOLDFINCH

Scientific Name: *Carduelis tristis*
Length: 5 inches (13 centimeters)
Year Made State Bird: 1935

American goldfinches love to eat seeds. Their favorites are thistle seeds. The goldfinches also like dandelions, aster, and goldenrod seeds.

Adult goldfinches feed their babies a steady diet of seeds, but first the parent swallows the seeds. The seeds soften into a "cereal" in the adult's stomach. Then the adult transfers the food to its nestlings.

(See Iowa, p. 17; and Washington, p. 44.)

New Mexico
Greater Roadrunner

Scientific Name: *Geococcyx californianus*
Length: 20 - 24 inches (50 - 60 centimeters)
Year Made State Bird: 1949

Unlike other members of the cuckoo family, the roadrunner loves to hustle about the ground. It is, indeed, a runner.

Roadrunners chase prey, which is often a snake or lizard. The roadrunner doesn't have a hooked beak, like a hawk, but it does have a long, sharp beak for jabbing.

Roadrunners like dry, open country. They are very much at home in New Mexico and much of the Southwest.

New York
Eastern Bluebird

Scientific Name: *Sialia sialis*
Length: 7 inches
   (18 centimeters)
Year Made State Bird: 1970

By making the bluebird its official state bird, New York helped people learn about the bluebird's troubles. By the mid 1960's, the bluebird had disappeared from many places where it had been common. Starlings were taking over nest holes in trees. Chemicals used to kill insects were working their way into the bodies of bluebirds and killing them.

The bluebird is making a comeback. Many insect-killing chemicals have been banned. In addition, efforts to provide birdhouses for bluebirds have helped. (See Missouri, p. 26.)

North Carolina
Cardinal

Scientific Name:
   Cardinalis cardinalis
Length: 7 1/2 - 9 inches
   (19 - 23 centimeters)
Year Made State Bird: 1943

(North Carolina continued)

North Carolina's state bird, the cardinal, is at home in a variety of habitats. It likes open woodlands, backyard shrubs, brush, and the thickets along fence rows.

Cardinals usually nest in bushes, thickets, or small trees. The nest is rarely more than 10 feet (3 meters) above the ground.

(See Illinois and Indiana, p. 16; Kentucky, p. 19; Ohio, p. 34; Virginia, p. 43; and West Virginia, p. 46.)

NORTH DAKOTA
WESTERN MEADOWLARK

Scientific Name:
Sturnella neglecta
Length: 9 inches
(23 centimeters)
Year Made State Bird:
1947

North Dakota's state bird, the western meadowlark, is common across the state. The prairies and fields of North Dakota are ideal habitats for this songster.

Farmers welcome western meadowlarks for their help in controlling insects that would otherwise eat crops.

North Dakota was the sixth state to adopt the western meadowlark as its state bird.

(See Kansas, p. 18; Montana, p. 26; Nebraska, p. 27; Oregon, p. 36; and Wyoming, p. 47.)

OHIO
CARDINAL

Scientific Name: *Cardinalis cardinalis*
Length: 7 1/2 - 9 inches (19 - 23 centimeters)
Year Made State Bird: 1933

In Ohio, as in many other northern states, cardinals are winter visitors to feeders. The growing use of feeders has probably helped the redbird widen its range in the northern states.

Cardinals eat a variety of feeder foods, but they seem to like sunflower seeds best.

(See Illinois and Indiana, p. 16; Kentucky, p. 19; North Carolina, p. 32; Virginia, p. 43; and West Virginia, p. 46.)

Oklahoma
Scissor-tailed Flycatcher

Scientific Name: *Muscivora forficata*
Length: 11 - 15 inches (28 - 38 centimeters)
Year Made State Bird: 1951

The beautiful and graceful scissor-tailed flycatcher catches insects in mid-air. It typically perches on a wire or post, then darts into action when an insect flies near.

Many kinds of flycatchers live in the United States. The scissor-tailed, named for its long tail feathers, is the largest kind found regularly in the United States. The scissor-tailed flycatcher lives in the south central U.S.

OREGON
WESTERN MEADOWLARK

Scientific Name:
Sturnella neglecta
Length: 9 inches
(23 centimeters)
Year Made State Bird:
1927

Oregon is a state of great forests, crashing ocean surf, and rugged mountains. It is also a state of plains and open farms. Its state bird, the western meadowlark, is at home in Oregon's fields and on its farms.

The meadowlark nests in the grass and finds bugs to eat in the grassy vegetation and soil.

(See Kansas, p. 18; Montana, p. 26; Nebraska, p. 27; North Dakota, p. 33; and Wyoming, p.47.)

PENNSYLVANIA
RUFFED GROUSE (PARTRIDGE)

Scientific Name:
Bonasa umbellus
Length: 16 - 19 inches
(40 - 48 centimeters)
Year Made State Bird:
1931

(Pennsylvania continued)

Pennsylvania's state bird, the ruffed grouse, is a popular game bird in the northern states and Canada. When startled, it bolts upward with a loud whirring of wings.

The grouse is a plump, chickenlike bird that spends much of its life on the ground. Its flights are short, low, and fast.

The male ruffed grouse attracts females each spring by rapidly beating its wings to make a loud rolling sound called "drumming."

Ruffed grouse live in the low, brushy parts of woodlands.

RHODE ISLAND
RHODE ISLAND RED HEN

Scientific Name:
   Gallus domesticus
Weight: 5 - 8 pounds
   (2.3 - 3.6 kilograms)
Year Made State Bird:
   1954

Rhode Islanders are proud of their red chickens. The Rhode Island Red is a famous breed developed in the state. The ancestors of modern Rhode Island Reds were chickens that a Rhode Island poultry farmer mated in 1854.

The new breed was a big improvement over breeds that existed in New England at that time. The Red was good for both egg-laying and meat.

The breed isn't as popular as it used to be because farmers prefer breeds that are outstanding for meat *or* eggs, not both.

SOUTH CAROLINA
CAROLINA WREN

Scientific Name:
Thryothorus ludovicianus
Length: 5 3/4 inches (14 centimeters)
Year Made State Bird: 1948

The Carolina wren loves thickets in yards and brushy areas where it hunts insects. Although it is South Carolina's state bird, it lives throughout the East and Midwest.

The Carolina wren is a singer all through the year. While many kinds of birds stop singing during the cold months, the Carolina wren continues its cheery song: *chirpity, chirpity, chirpity.*

SOUTH DAKOTA
RING-NECKED PHEASANT

Scientific Name:
Phasianus colchicus
Length: 30 - 36 inches (75 - 90 centimeters)
Year Made State Bird: 1943

(South Dakota continued)

South Dakota's state bird, the ring-necked pheasant, was unknown in the state until a hundred years ago. In the 1890's, the ring-necked pheasant was imported to South Dakota and other states from China.

The grain fields of South Dakota are ideal homes for this handsome game bird. The fields provide food, like corn, and the brushy edges provide hiding and nesting places.

The ring-neck has done well in many of the northern states. Hunters of this pheasant, one of the most popular game birds in America, consider South Dakota the best ring-neck state.

TENNESSEE

MOCKINGBIRD

Scientific Name:
Mimus polyglottos
Length: 9 - 11 inches
(23-28 centimeters)
Year Made State Bird:
1933

The mockingbird drew attention long before it became Tennessee's state bird. More than 200 years ago, Native Americans in the Southeast knew the mockingbird as the bird of "four hundred tongues." Its scientific name means "many-tongued mimic" or "imitator." (See Arkansas, p. 8; Florida, p.12; Mississippi, p. 25; and Texas, p. 40.)

TEXAS
MOCKINGBIRD

Scientific Name: *Mimus polyglottos*
Length: 9 - 11 inches (23 - 28 centimeters)
Year Made State Bird: 1927

Texans are proud of their state's great size. When Texans chose a state bird in 1927, though, they chose a small bird, known for its songs and calls.

The mockingbird imitates other birds. A "mocker" in Boston could mimic 39 different bird songs! In addition, it had its own calls.

Mockers were once sold as cage birds because of their delightful songs.

(See Arkansas, p. 8; Florida, p. 12; Mississippi, p. 25; and Tennessee, p. 39.)

UTAH

CALIFORNIA GULL (SEA GULL)

Scientific Name: *Larus californicus*
Length: 20 - 23 inches (50 - 58 centimeters)
Year Made State Bird: 1955

Utah's state bird is the California gull. In Utah, however, it's known simply as the "sea gull."

California gulls were honored as Utah's state bird because they helped Utah pioneers in 1848. When huge armies of grasshoppers threatened to eat all the pioneers' crops, thousands of hungry gulls swooped upon the grasshoppers and feasted.

California gulls nest in Utah. Many of them spend winters on the California coast, however.

41

VERMONT
HERMIT THRUSH

Scientific Name: *Catharus guttatus*
Length: 7 inches (18 centimeters)
Year Made State Bird: 1941

During the summer nesting season, Vermont's state bird is a hermit. It hides, usually out of sight, in dark evergreen forests. The bird's clear, flutelike call, heard at dawn and dusk, gives the hermit thrush away.

The hermit thrush usually nests and hunts on the ground. It picks through fallen leaves and needles to find beetles, ants, and caterpillars.

VIRGINIA
NORTHERN CARDINAL

Scientific Name: *Cardinalis cardinalis*
Length: 7 1/2 - 9 inches (19 - 23 centimeters)
Year Made State Bird: 1950

Virginia was the last of seven states that made the cardinal its state bird.

Today the cardinal is protected in Virginia and elsewhere. It was once a popular cage bird, however. The males were prized for their brilliant color and their cheerful song. (See Illinois and Indiana, p. 16; Kentucky, p. 19; North Carolina, p. 32; Ohio, p. 34; and West Virginia, p. 46.)

WASHINGTON

AMERICAN GOLDFINCH
(WILLOW GOLDFINCH)

Scientific Name: *Carduelis tristis*
Length: 5 inches (13 centimeters)
Year Made State Bird: 1967

So wide is the American goldfinch's range that it is a state bird on both American shores. New Jersey, on the Atlantic Coast, claims the American goldfinch as a state bird, and Washington on the Pacific Coast. Iowa, too, named the goldfinch its state bird.

Flocks of goldfinches visit feeders in winter. They are not easy to identify because both male and female are wearing brownish winter plumage, instead of summer gold. (See Iowa, p. 17; and New Jersey, p. 30.)

WASHINGTON, D.C.
WOOD THRUSH

Scientific Name: *Hylochichla mustelina*
Length: 8 inches (20 centimeters)
Year Made State Bird: 1967

Slightly smaller than its cousin the robin, another type of thrush, the wood thrush is a fine singer. It usually sings at dawn and dusk. A male wood thrush may greet another wood thrush with 10 minutes of nonstop melody!

Wood thrushes prefer woodlands, but they sometimes invade towns, wooded parks, and yards. The wood thrush's rusty brown back and spotted breast help it hide easily in dark, leafy habitats.

WEST VIRGINIA
CARDINAL

Scientific Name:
Cardinalis cardinalis
Length: 7 1/2 - 9 inches
(19 - 23 centimeters)
Year Made State Bird:
1949

A female cardinal, like her mate, has a crest, but not his brilliant color. Female cardinals are more the color of old red barns in need of paint.

A male cardinal is a fierce defender of its territory. Still, his efforts can't always keep away cats, snakes, owls, and cowbirds. Cowbirds lay their eggs in the nests of other birds. The big baby cowbirds crowd out the other bird's nestlings. (See: Illinois and Indiana, p. 16; Kentucky, p. 19; North Carolina, p. 32; Ohio, p. 34; and Virginia, p.43.)

WISCONSIN
AMERICAN ROBIN

Scientific Name:
Turdus migratorius
Length: 9 - 11 inches
(23 - 28 centimeters)
Year Made State Bird:
1949

(Wisconsin continued)

Wisconsin's state bird, the American robin, has no trouble existing near homes and gardens. They often nest in yards, choosing small trees or shrubs for their nests of mud, straw, and string.

Robins are protected by law today, but in earlier times they were slaughtered for sale in meat markets. John James Audubon, an American artist of birds, wrote in 1841 that winter robins were "fat and juicy, and afford excellent eating." (See Connecticut, p. 11; and Michigan p. 23.)

WYOMING

WESTERN MEADOWLARK

Scientific Name:
 Sturnella neglecta
Length: 9 inches
 (23 centimeters)
Year Made State Bird: 1937

The western meadowlark, Wyoming's state bird, can be found in the state's prairies, sagebrush flats, and Rocky Mountain grasslands. In summer these birds live as high as 12,000 feet (3,658 meters) above sea level.

Flocks of meadowlarks spend the winter as far north as they can find snow-free feeding areas.
(See Kansas, p. 18; Montana, p. 26; Nebraska, p. 27; North Dakota, p. 33; and Oregon, p. 36.)

INDEX